C000113509

Old Leigh Port Through Times of Change

Personal Stories and Reflections

Edited by:

Malcolm Jones

David Savill

Giles Tofield

Anna Patel

Peter Vadden

Carole Mulroney

2020 First Edition

Printed by
Leiston Press
Unit 1 -1b Masterlord Ind Est
Leiston
Suffolk
IP16 4JD
01728 833003
www.leistonpress.com

ISBN: 978-1-911311-63-8

Introductions

This book emerged from the 'Revealing the Maritime History of Leigh on Sea' project that ran through 2019 and into 2020. This formed the 'heritage' part of the 'North Thames Fisheries Local Action Group' (or NTFLAG) that was an EU funded programme to address a number of important infrastructure challenges in Old Leigh - challenges that if not dealt with could have undermined the future prosperity of the Port of Leigh-on-Sea and with it a 1000 years of maritime and fishing history.

The NTFLAG was a partnership between Thames Estuary Partnership and the Cultural Engine and many other organisations. The funding was important, but bringing people together to take positive action was the most important thing. So many people have a connection to Old Leigh for many different reasons – family history, business and visitors. 2016 – 2020 was a critical time for the Port; a time for making the case for investment in energy, wharves, creeks and heritage to secure the Port's future. Alongside this process however there was a clear sense that Leigh's future was very closely aligned with its past.

The personal memories recorded in this book provide a unique insight into Old Leigh – feelings, experiences, thoughts, reflections and laughs. The memories and personal connections to the place all go back decades (and well before that through family). Some participants were keen not only to tell their own story but that of parents and grandparents which helped recreate a picture of Leigh between the wars, during the Second World War and into the 50s and 60s. Everyone who came forward to be interviewed witnessed the Port during times of major change, and they have all made contributions and played important roles. Some of them are 'outsiders' and some are 'Leighites' born and bred. The memories and personal reflections are not meant to represent factual history or chronological accounts of names and events. Other books have recorded this. There are of course many other people who have important links to Old Leigh, so this is not an exhaustive account of personal memories. In creating the book Cultural Engine and Leigh Heritage Centre have worked closely with Age Exchange specialists in oral history. Age Exchange carried out the interviews with all those who contributed their personal and family histories. We are grateful to all the participants who have kindly enabled us to use photographs from their family collections in the book.

Personal stories and family histories are so important to record and to share. Through them we can learn about community and social history from those who have lived at the heart of the community and who, along with their families past and present, have contributed so much to it. We are all looking forward to a prosperous future for Leigh Port.

Giles Tofield – Director, Cultural Engine CIC

Leigh is a very special place and has a very special history, but more often than not it is the history of the ordinary folk who have lived and worked here for years that brings to light the fascination we all have for the town.

This book is just one example of the pride and pleasure we have in Leigh and which we want to see preserved for future generations.

Carole Mulroney
Chairman, North Thames Fisheries Local Action Group and of the Trustees of Leigh Heritage Centre

DARRYL GODBOLD

My mother's side of the family were all bargeman, they were called the Cornwalls and came from Barling and Wakering. When I was 10 or 12 in the mid-1950s I used to go out with my Uncle George and go aboard the barge. They used to unload at the loading pier in Southend next to the gas line. They were mainly bringing timber, bricks, grain and flour. But my father's family were not water people. He was a carpenter or joiner. He met my mum pre-war about 1928. My mother's family had been wildfowlers or marsh men in the early days, living off the land. They were semi-farmers and whatever came up they turned their hand to it in order to live.

My grandfather was in the Salvation Army and was Bandmaster at Southchurch. He was called Cornelius Cornwall. I was born in 53a Belllevue Road Southend and we moved to Old Southend Road, which is up near the Kursaal. Of course I was playing on the beach all the time.

When I was a boy alongside the east side of Southend Pier there must have been nearly 20 full time fishermen but they are all gone now. There used to be Guy and Harry Wilkinson and all the Gilsons. There were the Thomas', there was Les and Eric Thomas and their father William Thomas. I worked for them in my early days. There was another relation called Sam Thomas, whose father was originally the coxswain of the Southend Lifeboat. Sam passed it on to Peter Gilson in the 1950s that was the big boat, The Greater London. I did some time on that in the 1960s.

The big fishing families were the Thomas', the Gilsons, the Polkinghorns; there was a chap called Frank Carling and another called Freddie Plappett. They all began their fishing career after the Second World War. Of course we as young boys thought fishing was a great way to turn a penny in those days.

When I was even younger and lived in Southend Road on Saturday mornings I used to do the 'coke run'. We would take out an old pram and go out to the gasworks and you would put two of three hundredweight of coke for the neighbours and push it up and down the hill for them and you made sixpence.

I went to Southchurch School and I left school when I was 15. But from about 14 I worked for the Thomas' in the summer holidays and times like that and if I wasn't working for them I was working for the Pleasure Boat men along the Southend sea front. They were people like Dick Murrell with the Dreadnought or Albert Brand on the Prince of Wales. I was like a third hand and doing jobs like rowing the boat about for them or putting ropes on the bigger boats.

My first wage working for the Thomas's was about £3.10 shillings.

When we were older and started to go fishing it was for dover sole, skate and sprats in the winter time. There's not been a lot of change in that respect actually as that is still the predominant fish around here. The fish in the River Thames is all migratory and it comes in with the season. In the winter there are sprats, herrings, a few whitings or dabs or a few cod. Summertime you get dover sole, plaice, skate, bass, mullet, sometimes the odd bream or the odd turbot. But the high quality fish here was Dover Sole.

The cockle industry was different to the fishing industry. There wasn't enough hours in the day to do both jobs. There were actually a couple of men who did both, there was Fred Cotgrove and Bob Osborne who used to go out on the Crusader. But most of the people I mentioned would be fishing all year round. Most boats just had a skipper and a boy. My skipper was Harry Thomas, who was a Salvation Army man. Most of the skippers were fairly upright citizens. Some like Frank Carling or Fred Plappett had come out of the Second World War where they may have been doing things like mine-laying duties. We all cut corners a bit because there was so little money and you did your best to keep your boat running.

Later I worked for Eric Thomas and his father William Thomas. The younger son Les built his boat here in Seacraft in what is now a restaurant. But all the boats were built here by a man called Frank Parsons. There a few built on Strand Wharf and a few at Johnson and Jago's. There were a couple of smaller ones like Sea Kings but they built yachts rather than fishing boats. I had the Stormdrift, then I came back here and had the Megan. I had gone away for 8 years and worked out of Lowestoft on deep sea fishing. Then I bought the Twilight Star, which I just sold two years ago after I had her for 36 years.

I worked 5 years for the Thomas's and it was like being an apprentice. I was taught how to make nets and some mechanical engineering, really everything a person needed to survive in that industry. Then I saved and saved and eventually bought myself a little boat and I progressed from there. I have had five boats since I started fishing. I became a skipper at about 20 and my first boy was Len Cooper. He was just 15 and he was off and on with me for quite a few years. He lived just around the corner from me. He and his dad used to come rod and line angling with me and it progressed from there. He was a good hand and the last time he was working here he was cockling for the Osbornes but he still comes out with me now and must be 54 now.

Most of my fish went to London although I used to serve a few locals. I live in Hadleigh and behind me lived a chap called Roger Barton who was on television. He was a fish merchant at Billingsgate but he was often on TV programmes. I used to serve him for the best part of 40 years and he was a character and a 100% genuine.

We all found our own place to fish I used to do a lot of fishing around Leigh because you could work longer in bad weather. So I exploited a bit of land round here and cleaned it up, removing old anchors and wreckage over the years. But you kept that information to yourself. Anyone could work on anyone's territory but you didn't go and tread on people's toes because you didn't do yourself any favours. In reality you were better off with one boat fishing in one place as if there were too many boats you would over-fish it and then no one got a good day's work. So you did a circle and avoided fishing on the same piece of ground so it got a rest. The thing with fishing is it was 'little and often'. You might have your big catches but what you really wanted was a steady catch through the day. If you had 40 or 50 soles a haul then you had got a day's work. There was no point in getting a bigger haul and nothing the next day. You wanted to get 4 or 5 good hauls, that's how it worked. Then you sold them but the restaurants here only wanted big soles so you could end up with two or three boxes you couldn't sell. Whereas Roger Barton, who I mentioned before, would buy everything. He would put it on his van to Billingsgate and he would sell the full range, everything from 9 and a half inch fish to 20 inch fish and I wouldn't be left with anything.

I was also lucky because the woman I married was a fishmonger's daughter who had wet and dry fish shops, in fact that's how I met her, because I supplied her father with cod in the 1960s. He was a gentleman and he took my fish. There weren't many people at that time who had fridges to store fish but he let me take my fish up at any time of the day or night and just put a note of them to say could he please take them to Billingsgate. In that way I didn't have to worry because he went up every Tuesday, Thursday and Saturday morning. So my fish was there at 5.00am in the morning.

I have seen a lot of changes in the way we fish. When I first started a lot of young men from Leigh and Southend were all on beam trawls. That is a long beam with a net attached that keeps its spread. But then what we called the Otter Trawl came in from Belgium and was named after a chap called Otter. Most of the Southend boats took that up first. It had a set of doors that spread the nets. The boats I worked on were all Otter Trawling boats. We also had a couple of boats whitebaiting and that was the Saxonia and the Enterprise. As a young man I went on them and that was called Stow Boating. What you used to do was to lay two big wooden baulks over the front of the boat and the net was attached to them. One part of the baulk was attached to your anchor and when you lowered your anchor your net would go down with it and it would hold it front of the boat in a square and then you just lay it to tide and the small whitebait swim into it.

But that's all gone now since we became mechanical. When I first came into fishing the engines were very small and 30 horsepower was a big engine in the late 1950s. But now they are up to two or three hundred horsepower so you can see how things progressed. Maybe it was all too fast for what was really a small cottage industry. The river has also been cleaned up but a funny thing is that as the river became cleaner the fish stock seems to have declined. It seems that some of the effluent actually fed fish. At one time what we called the Bovril Boats came down from Tilbury and discharged the sewerage in the outer end of the estuary and we noticed when they stopped the fish stocks started to deteriorate.

Over the years the industry started to die. It was like a man had a three cornered hat and he would turn the hat one way to do one job and another way to do another job. But that was all taken away from us. The pressures put on us by the powers above through the quota system didn't allow us the leeway to catch the fish. For instance when the cod comes here in the autumn most of the cod quota had already been caught so we couldn't fish them.

The Leigh and Southend fisherman have always been reliant on seasonal fish but if the big fishing industry outside the six or twelve mile limit fished very hard during the winter time that meant there was a lack of fish coming into the estuary.

You have to remember that it wasn't only Leigh and Southend that had fishing boats when I was younger. There were boats at Whitstable, Faversham, Margate, Ramsgate, Queenborough and West Mersea. When I first stated there were an awful lot of fishermen on the Thames. In 1992 it was recorded that there were 161 boats, now there's about 30.

I would say it's a young man's job. I retired when I was 68 and I'm 74 now. It's 12 or 14 hours a day on your feet, so hard work. Sometimes you started at 12.00 at night and not finish until 3.00pm in the afternoon. In fact the last 5 years I worked single-handed as there wasn't enough money in the industry. The cockle industry has done better than the fishing industry over the last few years for sure.

But I always wanted to be a boatman or a fisherman that was my aim in life, so things like getting up early was never a problem for me. When I left Secondary School one of my teachers wrote on my leaving exam 'If this boy took as much notice of his schooling as he does of fishing boats he would be brilliant'

There are a lot of families involved in the industry and of course we all knew each other. There was the Ford brothers, Georgie and Tony. There was Peter Belton, who had a boat called the Reminder and Teddy Potter, who had the Sarastro, and China Cotgrove, who had the Boy David. There was also Dennis Brown on the Rainbow and Ivan had the Marjorie Nora. A lot of them have left but I still see some of the old characters coming along the High Street.

It could be dangerous work but you do acquire a bit of foresight and doing the job every day you recognise the pitfalls and make sure you avoid them. The main problem if you are on your own was if you had your net down and caught an anchor or even sometimes an old mine from the war. There were still mines around and I had three magnetic mines and a spike mine catch the net. You just raised them and saw what it was and gently lowered it back down. Then you called the Port of London Authority and they would arrange for bomb disposal to come and take them away.

The weather is another thing to be respectful of. I have been out on a beautiful day and the weather has deteriorated so quickly so you always think about it and make decisions based on your knowledge. There were very few ship to shore radios when I started. The first man to start making them was a chap called Jack Spratt. He lived on Southchurch Avenue and he had been a radio operator during the war. He started building these sets called Ajax sets which were very fine radios. But some of the blokes bought ex-Government surplus stuff like Tank radios.

Over the years I have done quite a lot to challenge the Government legislation on fishing and its effect on this community. The last thing I did was organise the flotilla in 2016 to object to EU control of our industry.

Looking back I would do it all again. I loved the freedom to do what I wanted. I was very lucky I did what I wanted and I made my living out of it. But I wouldn't want to do it in the present situation. The people who are supposed to be in charge of our industry have not been fishermen. So there's a lot of understanding lacking. You cannot teach the unteachable because they don't want to listen. I have stood in front of minister after minister since 1973 and all I have heard is "I'm sorry Mr Godbold but I can't do anything for you because Europe won't let me".

STEVE MEDDLE

My family history goes back quite a long way and I come from a fishing family. When I first started in the business it was with my granddad and then my father and my uncle. They were all cockle fishermen for generations back to the 19th Century. I first went out on a boat when I was probably 5 or 6 years old. I left school in 1970, I think I was 15, which was the school leaving age then. Straightaway I went out on a boat called Ranger II; they were wooden boats then. The actual cockling was just on the changeover then from hand raking to the suction dredgers.

I had done a little bit of hand raking, not a lot, so mainly my career has been cockle dredging. Hand raking was completely different. You had to go out on the ebb tide and take the ground. Then wait till the tide went out and go over the side with the rakes and hand nets, and then you would hand rake the cockles into nets and then tip the cockles into baskets. Then they were brought back aboard the vessel and then when the tide came in brought back to Leigh for processing. The cockles weren't processed on the boat but back in Leigh. For many years the unloading was always done with yokes and baskets. So, it was very labour intensive when you landed the cockles. From our mooring to where our cockle shed was the longest distance, which made it even worse! We had someone come down to help us unload, but it still took each of us many trips each from the boat to the shed, as you only carry two baskets at a time, and there would be about 250 baskets. I tell you I used to be 6 foot 6 inches before I carried cockle baskets. Knowing the tides was something you got brought up with, and you knew exactly if they are going to be big tides or small tides on prediction or the winds too and you take all that into consideration. But you always go by the forecast.

As you are working mainly inside the estuary the problem you can get is small, sharp, choppy waves rather than long rollers but anywhere can be dangerous on the water especially the mud banks, you need to be careful or the boat can get grounded. Everyone had an experience when the bilge pumps packed up especially on the wooden boats and you were taking on water and the seas were coming over the top. But you just did what you had to do, even bailing out with buckets. One thing is the forecasts now are much more realistic than they used to be and you have more equipment. But you need to have a lot of respect for water.

So when I left school I went straight aboard the boat. At that time there were three of us on the boat, there was myself, my uncle and another crew member. Then after a few months it was myself and my uncle. It was just a done deal that I would be on the boats. Every summer holiday when I was at school and every weekend I was always down on the boats and in the cockle sheds. Sometimes cooking with my granddad, my dad and my uncle, so from a very early age I have always been involved in the cockle industry.

My father's boats were smaller boats than we have now. But they built the business up with bigger boats. But to be honest it hadn't changed much for years apart from modernisation. The biggest change was, as I have said, from hand raking to dredging. Our boat was called Ranger II which was the first boat to experiment with these cockle dredgers.

Most people around here had nicknames, my granddads nickname was 'Itty'. I don't even know how he got it, he was just 'Itty' but they all had them. Mine was 'Itty 2'. I think it was just a thing people did over the years and that's what they were known by. So in the end it was just me and my Uncle on the boat which was enough for the dredging side of it. We were out all sorts of times depending on the time of the tides. Sometimes we were out overnight and then you might stay out for 30 or 36 hours but a normal day would be about 14 hours. You would work with somebody for a long while so you got used to being with them.

I became skipper when I was 16 and I had a friend who I got to be my crew and we were together for about 4 years. I was married quite young and my wife came from an old town family. We lived in Theobald's Cottages in Old Leigh for a couple of years. So I used to go one way to work and another to the pub which was The Smack. Her granddad was a fisherman and worked on the Whitebait boats.

It was a good life but how good depended on the weather. In the winter it was often blowing hard and cold and we didn't have a wheelhouse on my old boat and it was just a tiller. So you were outside with no shelter and in the winter you thought 'Oh mate!' We had oilskins, big old yellow oilskins and they were stiff as boards. We would make a time to go out and my mate would turn up. We would take out a fry up on the boat with stove. Now we have ovens and microwaves and take modern food. But it was a skill cooking on the boat especially when the weather was bad, and you were trying to fry an egg and it was roaring around the pan doing 90 mile an hour!

When I first started there was no navigation equipment. We didn't even have an echo sounder. We used to use a lead line, which was a piece of lead on the bottom of a rope, and you used to chuck it in the water and it was marked off with fathoms so you used to measure out the depth with that. But the equipment we have now is computers, VHF radios, echo sound, radars so it's a big difference.

We also used to go white weeding sometimes. It's quite unique to this part of the river and it's a bit like a soft coral. In its heyday it could be a big money earner for the processors. They used to wash it and dye it and sell it in small coloured bunches for things like fish tanks, or as ornaments or even to decorate coffins. The fishermen used to go out with weed rakes and chuck them over the back of the boat and run the teeth across the seabed and then haul it up, then you would take off the white weed and carry on the process again. They still fish for it but it's not in such great demand.

We have done many types of fishing over the years including oysters, mussels and shrimps and trawling. Cockling was a very hard living. Over the years I have been doing it there were good years and bad years so it was very up and down. Just when you think you are having a reasonable spell you get two or three bad years which really knocks you back a peg or two. It could be many reasons for that, perhaps the cockles aren't there, the market, the prices or the demand.

When I first started all the processing would be done by hand, there was a big old steam boiler fed by coal and that produced steam to pressure pots which we used to put the cockles in to be steamed. Now everything is done by machine and they go in one end and come out the other end all done. As soon as they are boiled or steamed the shells open and the meat and the shell is tipped on to a sieve and the sieve needs to be the right size mesh to let the right size cockles through. The meat falls through into a holding tank and the shells are discarded. In the old days they were put around the back of the sheds and there used to be massive great piles of cockleshells. One of the worst jobs was to have to get on top of the pile of shells and shovel another hole for the next lot of shells to go in. There used to be a company who came and took the shells away. At one time there was a crushing shed down here and they would be used for chicken feed but that's all gone. The shells now are used for drainage and golf club pathways. Also now because of Health and Safety the shells have to be taken away every day whereas years ago they would just lie at the back of the shed for quite a while.

Now my youngest son is the skipper of the Indiana and Boy Michael. I have taken on a bit more of the shore side of things and maintenance etc. In one respect compared to my time the fishing side of it and the boat side of it is much easier but it's the paperwork, we have to have electronic logbooks so it is much more involved in that respect. If I had the chance I would do it all again but then again it was all I knew. I couldn't have commuted up to London that's for sure.

COLIN SEDGWICK MBE

I joined the 3rd Chalkwell Bay Sea Scouts when I was about 11 years old. I played a very active part in the Sea Scouts and finished up as the Patrol Leader of the Stormy Petrels. Ray Hopkins and myself were the first people to get our Queen's Scouts Awards in the 3rd Chalkwell Bay when we were about 15, I am 77 years old now. I finished up as a scout master with 3rd Chalkwell Bay for Rodney Troop and Nelson Troop for about 7 or 8 years.

The Sea Scouts used to be on the other side of the Railway where the footbridge is now, next to The Bell Hotel. Then we bought a building off the Salvation Army, and we took it to bits and rebuilt it on that bit of land on the other side of the railway. It had 44 pillars, and we built the pillars out of 5 gallon drums with cement in them. That was masterminded under a chap called Dick Harris, who used to live at the top of Leigh Hill, next to Captain McCraith, who was an elder brethren of Trinity House, who opened what was called The Den. Then we moved to Victoria Wharf and we re-built it there, and then after a period of time they moved on to building a new premises, although I had gone to run the Lifeboats by then. My children were all in the Sea Scouts at that time, and quite a lot of the 3rd Chalkwell Bay Sea Scouts from Leigh came along as crew members on the Lifeboat when I started. Even today there are 4 crew members at Southend Lifeboat that come from 3rd Chalkwell Bay.

I was also involved in the Greater London Sea Scouts; I was Charge Examiner for the London River and I used to pass out Sea Scouts from the London area. While I was scoutmaster at 3rd Chalkwell Bay I used to run training weekends on HMS Discovery which I could do because I was an Examiner. The HMS Discovery was moored on the Victoria Embankment in London and was used for London Sea Scout training.

I also got involved in running the London Sea Scouts meet during Whitsun half term each year for 5 years at Chatham Dockyard. We had 2,500 scouts at the Whitsun meets and I looked after the boating side of it with my wife, Lesley. We have now been married for over 50 years. We have 4 children, all boys and two of them work in the family business, Mike's Boatyard Ltd.

When I started in the Lifeboat Service (RNLI), I was aged about 15 or 16, rowing the ropes out to get the lifeboat back on the slipway, I was about 16 when I started going out on the lifeboats. When I first joined the Lifeboats, it was the Greater London Lifeboat Crew, which worked with the old Watson Lifeboat, that was an 8 knot lifeboat, where I was on the crew of eight men. When we started the Inshore Lifeboats, they became the D Class rubber boats. I was the youngest and was interested in promoting them. I took over running the Inshore Lifeboats for the RNLI in Southend, and I carried on and moved up the tree until I was the Operations Manager, and I retired at the age of 70; because you have to retire at 70. For me it was the right time to retire, as I had to have open heart surgery at that time, and when you are on duty 24 hours a day, and with so much crew to manage it was enough. So, I retired from that and I came back to the boatyard full time working with my children.

In the Lifeboat service I ended up with a Gold Badge and a Double Bar. In 2012, I received an MBE for my services to Maritime Safety including my service to the town and the Thames Estuary. I was involved in the RNLI for 54 years.

I went from being in the boat to running the station. So a lot of my time has been in charge of running the station at Southend. We ended up with one Atlantic 21; now an Atlantic 85, two D Class Lifeboats and a Hovercraft. I was really keen on the Hovercraft because we had so much mud at Southend, which made it hard to reach some casualties. Then my final project at Southend Lifeboat Station was building the new Inshore Lifeboat House; we had fought for over 8 years to have that built. This Lifeboat House houses the D Class ILB, and the Hovercraft. The crew also now have a warm room and a shower and places to dry all their equipment, and carry out training etc.

I arranged two visits for Princess Anne for the RNLI at Southend, the first was on the 2nd May 1986 when HRH named the new Atlantic 21 Lifeboat 'Percy Garon' and the new Pier trains. Later that year on the 30th June 1986 the boat 'Kings Abbey' went through the neck of the Pier and impaled itself in the Lifeboat slipway. The Lifeboat House was so badly damaged it had to be demolished. The Lifeboat from the end of the Pier was re-stationed in Mike's Boatyard Ltd in Old Leigh and launched from Two Tree Island on a tractor and trailer until the temporary Lifeboat House was built at the end of the Pier. During these times, without a lifeboat house, we had to initiate a Leigh-on-Sea launching crew who lived in the immediate area of Old Leigh who used to take the tractor and lifeboat to Two Tree Island, and launch it for the crew. When the temporary Lifeboat House was established at the end of Southend Pier, Princess Anne came for the second time and opened the temporary Boathouse. At that time I was running the annual Southend raft race in aid of the RNLI - this ran for 15 years.

We also had experiences like the Pier fire. It didn't damage the boat but as the crew were trying to launch the boat to save it the fire burnt the back of their necks. But the boat was saved so it could be used.

So, I feel like I've seen it all. I'm Vice President but my only real involvement now is running the Life Boat Crews Dinner for over 400 people each year.

My youngest son Timothy was a Helmsman in the Lifeboat Service and so was my second son, Robin. Jonathan was away at University at that time and then came back to run the Boatyard. He is now a DLA (Deputy Launching Authority) and carries out some of the duties that I used to do in the Lifeboats at Southend.

I started life as a fisherman when I was 15. I used to work on a boat called the Teal. The Teal was owned by a man called Fred Cotgrove, who used to be called Gummy. His father had been a fisherman, and we worked out of Bell Wharf. We used to come in and he used to sell the fish to people on the quayside. It then went to fish shops. We were the only boat working out of Bell Wharf at that time. When we caught lobsters, I remember selling them to Jack Mayo at the Peterboat pub.

A few years after that we palled up with a chap called Bob Osborne, and a chap called Bobby Danks, his son; who at that point owned the Crusader. So, we used to pair fish with them and a little while after that we got involved with the Gilson family in Southend. We then worked with the Gilsons for quite a few years. They had five or six boats and we worked together as a team as that made more sense.

During that time the Teal sunk twice, she was quite a narrow boat that Fred had built. We were loaded to the gunnels with scraps once, off of Southend pier. She came around the inside of the pier, and she touched the ground, we couldn't get her off and she filled up with water and sank. We then pumped her out, lifted her up and got her up and running. On another occasion she broke her mooring at Southend and ended up under the pier wedged on her side, between the Gilsons and us we managed to get her out with blocks and tackle. She should never have come out but she did and it floated and she was recovered again.

As part of the Boatyard we also had a white weed factory. We would wash and process white weed. Eventually that came to an end as the demand for it dropped. Back in the Boatyard, we used to own a Cockle Boat called the Paula-Marie and we went Cockling with a chap called Mike Headford, who I was in partnership with originally in Mike's Boatyard. Then I parted company with Mike and bought the

Boatyard completely.

All my four children have worked at the Boatyard, sometimes on and off during the holidays. They were 10 or 11 years old, when they were first working in the shop. In 1984 Old Leigh saw a lot of building and the Council lifted the Boatyard and made that a sea wall. Eventually we decided it was time to sell.

Mike's Boatyard Ltd opened in 1970 and we just looked after boats and acted as a chandlery, but then the internet came along and strangled the chandlers' trade. At that time there were six chandlers in the Southend area and now there's none, which tells its own story. We then closed the chandlers but already had Theobalds Wharf and at that time Timothy my youngest son had been working in the boatyard with me and he ran the cockle stall next to the shop, he also used to look after the boats. The Boatyard was doing all sorts of jobs with boats but again things changed and fibreglass boats came along. The wooden boats disappeared and they became steel. So really anyone could learn to weld steel but not everyone could learn to work wood. Eventually the old yard closed and is now a restaurant. Now nearly all the people in Old Leigh have their own welders and we just help with the more complicated work or if it's a big job then my son Jonathan does it and he is a highly qualified and skilful engineer. Timothy is a welder and also skippers a Cockle Boat. We eventually moved all of the operations to the Theobalds Wharf area where we operate from today, with offices and workshops adjacent.

Colin, Jonathan and Timothy Sedgwick – Mike's Boatyard 2016

We now own three of the old cockle boats. One is in very good condition and is working and another is being rebuilt at the moment. We also own the fireworks barge that is used for a lot of the winter firework celebrations around the pier and the seafront. We supply the barge and service it and ferry it around and a firework company provides the fireworks.

So gradually the boatyard has developed, and it now carries out all marine trades including working up and down the Thames Estuary and the Medway, and all jetties surrounding the Estuary including Victoria Embankment London. My son Jonathan now runs Mike's Boatyard Ltd and associated companies.

PETER WEXHAM

I was always around boats since I was a kid. Growing up around here we would go out and play around the little dykes and creeks. It was just by where the station is now but it's all filled in today. We would ride our bikes over there and take a jam jar on a piece of string and catch tadpoles and newts and all sorts of things in the spring.

After I left school there was a gang of us who all joined up to the Merchant Navy. I did couple of trips but it wasn't for me.

So I came back ashore. Getting work on the boats was all about knowing someone. A friend said to me, did I know Roy Frost was looking for a mate. So I went down and knocked on his door and he said "Are you ready to start?" I said 'yes' and he said "Be around here at 7.00pm tonight". And this was about 3.00pm in the afternoon.

So that was my first experience on a fishing boat. It was what they called a Bawley. The original Bawleys were used as Shrimpers and for whitebait fishing. In Leigh there were about 5 big boiler houses so they could bring the shrimps in, get them cooked then onto the railway and up to London. But we used to have the boilers on the boats too. But Bawley boats didn't only fish for shrimp so the name relates to the boats rather than having boilers onboard .

In August it was the closed season for whitebait and there were two boats the Saxonia and The Enterprise and they would come into Bell Wharf here and lay up and being repainted and have all the work that needed to be done before they were ready to go out again. Whitebait was fished with nets. The Bawleys had great big anchors, big as a barge anchor. So you would drop the anchor and then drop the beams down with the anchor chain. There was one that floated and one that was weighted so it opened up the net. It was a great square net and then you just sit and wait out the tide and hope for the best.

There were two boats. One belonged to Young's who are now very famous for producing fish for supermarkets. The family lived in Leigh and set the company up here. He had a factory in Corringham and the shrimp boats would catch the shrimps and supply Youngs. They used to call Mr Young 'The Peeler' because he would take

William (Joe) Deal on Board the Endeavour

all these shrimps from Leigh and he had people working all around places like Basildon and Pitsea. He would deliver the shrimps to them and they would have to peel them all and then they would go into a pot of Young's Potted Shrimps.

Roy Frost and I worked for Myalls and we had to get the fish into them early in the morning because they had to get in on a train to Billingsgate Market in London so it arrived as fresh as possible. So we had to start work at about 5 or 6 o'clock in the evening to get the catch in and get the tide in and get it all done and cleaned to get it on the first train in the morning.

There would be two of us on the boat and of course, a lot of the time is spent doing nothing and waiting. You are walking up and down the deck. I was with Roy who was a funny old character. He was more of my father's generation. Through the night he would chew tobacco and spit it out and I remember he was always rolling fags. His daughter Maureen and my first wife, Brenda Deal, were good friends and lived close to each other. Well then one day, Brenda's father Joe said to me that his mate had just packed up because of his health and why didn't I go shrimping with him. He said it had more variety and you get more money. I was just getting a wage of about £4.10 shillings a week whereas with shrimping, there might be good times and bad times but you got your share of the catch. Whatever the boat earned was divided three ways, one for the skipper, one for the boat and one for the mate.

So then I went and worked on the Endeavour with Joe Deal, who were a big fishing family in Leigh. Joe's real name was William Deal but he was called Joe as a nickname after his father.

Shrimpers went out at night as you still worked on the tides. So you might go out at midnight or one o'clock in the morning and work through catching the shrimps usually over on the Kent coast. If you got a lot of shrimp you would come back and lay up in a mooring in the Leigh Ray. You cleaned and cooked the shrimps as you went along. There were about 14 shrimp boats in Leigh when I was working and then there were boats like the Endeavour and the Diana-Lou, which were cockle boats converted into shrimp boats. There was also about 15 cockleboats in the 60s. They were bigger than the shrimpers. The shrimp boats were made so you could work single-handed. It meant you could steer the boat and do all you needed to do like

14

cook the shrimps as you went along. But in the bigger cockle boats the cooking was in the hold so you couldn't do both. Of course it was hard work but all the years I worked with Joe, I would have done it for nothing. Getting paid as well was like a bonus I just loved it so much. It was just wonderful. I had no worries or cares. I enjoyed catching the shrimps, cleaning them and cooking them.

We would all go down to Billet Wharf and watch the weather especially if it was a bit blowy, we would get there about an hour's ebb. If it was rough you would stand there talking and watch the tide go out and then go back to bed or you would watch it and someone would say "I think it's OK". Then once one went out everybody would go or we would all stand there talking and trying to talk each other into either going or not going. It was all very friendly. Everybody helped everybody else. If someone was in trouble you would go alongside their boat and give them a bit of help.

The old boys like Joe Deal or Joe Becket used to sing hymns when they were out working. You could hear them in the fog. If it was a rough old night and I was going out with Joe I'd go down the cabin and make the tea. There would be water coming over the top and he would be singing at the tiller 'For Those in Peril on the Sea' and hymns like that.

There was another old boy who lived along the road here called Leslie Tommer. His father was 'Old Tommer', he worked in the Osborne's sheds picking out whelks and things for them. When he got old he was completely bent over and that's because in his younger days he used to go off in a skiff and go winkling off Canvey Point. He would have sacks full of winkles and wet sand on his back. He would have to carry that half a mile back to his boat and then row that back in. In those day I don't suppose they did anything to help him so he was completely bent over. He looked alright sitting down but he was in the same position when he stood up.

There were lots of characters, there was Ted Little whose nickname was 'Bedbug' as he was the last to get out of bed and down to the boats. He would just catch the tide before it went. He would say "You can't call me that". But they all had nicknames. I think it was a way of differentiating them as the first child was usually called after the father so all the Deals were called Joe or Joseph and The Bridges were the same, the boys were all called John. So they might call them John and 'Little John' It was the same with the Cotgroves or the Emerys they all had nicknames. Doug Emery had a boat called the Sylvia May and his nickname was 'Speed'. They used to say he had only got one speed and that was dead slow. There was another Stevie Lawrence, whose mother was an Osborne, and who is just a bit younger than me. He was called 'Beano' that was because when he was a kid all the brothers would go out and help on the boats. They would get a bit of pocket money for it and his mum would pack him up a box with his grub in and he always had his Beano comic in there to read. So it stuck and people would say 'Beano's down the cabin' and he is still called 'Beano' today.

Anyway after I got married to Brenda I went up to work at Thames Haven for a while, up at the Oil Refineries as I got more money. So then Brian Woods went out to help Joe. He used to work on what we called the Bovril Boats. They used to load up at Deptford Sewerage works. They would load up with sludge take in down the river to Black Deep and dump it and go back again. They called them Bovril Boats because when all the sewerage came out the water went a brown colour like a cup of Bovril.

It was a tight community around here. But if you went up to try to get a job at Tilbury it was hard as the Lightermen all had their own Association and it was handed on father to son.

Of course things changed over the years. One important thing was in the early 1960s the plastic nets came in. They were Corlene nets, which is a plastic. Before that they were cotton nets. With them you had to boil them up in the copper and then dry the nets to try to preserve the cotton otherwise it rotted very quickly. Whereas Corlene didn't rot of course, although what we found out as time went on was that like all plastics it was fine and flexible when you got it but as it gets older the sunlight or ultra violet light on it makes it go dry and crack and break.

In about 1968 Joe Deal died and as I was his son in law I took over the boat. Then we also did things like white weeding. Every boat in the area was going white weeding but Joe said 'I'm not giving up my shrimping to go white weeding'. But as time went on it got harder and harder and you needed extra money and you couldn't afford that time off in the winter and you needed something to do as the shrimps don't last all year around. As a fishermen you had the soles in the spring and then the shrimps in the summer and autumn. So then in the winter we went white weeding.

We could sell it in two or three places almost all the time and most of it went to America or Japan. It's like a fern. For a while it was the 'in thing' to have and fishermen had haystacks of it in the boat. They would get back to the shore where the bloke was waiting to take it and weigh it. One of things they did was put it in a bag and drop it in the water so it rehydrated and then when it was weighed it would be heavier!

In 1970 Dave Spurgeon and I entered the Trawler Race. It started at the end of

Peter winning the 1970 Trawler Race on Endeavour

Southend Pier and went up to Canvey Point then all the way back down south to Shoebury then back up again and round and back to the start at the Pier shore. Of course there were big boats and little boats, big engines and small engines so they had to handicap us. But we were first boat away and first boat home so we won the cup. It was a lot of fun and boats came from Harwich and Rye and Folkestone. It could get a bit competitive and some of them would upgrade the diesel engines so more diesel goes through and you go a bit faster. But the problem was some of them were like coal burners with black smoke coming out and blowing the exhausts apart!

GRAHAM DENT

Originally my family lived in Highlands Boulevard, Leigh, which is at the top of the hill. I went to school at West Leigh Infants School and prior to that I went to a Mrs Hall who had a house just around the corner from us where she educated children at 4 or 5 years old. Things were a bit hard in those days and Mrs Hall produced a box containing a number of coloured pencils and we would pick out the ones we needed and draw coloured pictures. Mrs Hall had to close for a while when her house had a near miss during the war. It must have been a near miss as it took our windows out. Then I went to West Leigh Infant School and in those days we used to walk to school and not necessarily with our parents with us either. I remember a milkman would come around in his horse drawn cart, which was replaced by a sleigh if there was snow on the ground. Things were very local and there were little jobs I did to help out like cycle to the butchers every Saturday morning to buy meat, which was with ration books of course. Our house was 103 Highlands Boulevard and the butchers was basically just around the corner but in the way were brick fields so you had to divert around those. So although as the crow flies it was a fairly short journey it was reasonably long one for a child of about 8 on a bicycle. After Primary School I went to Westcliff High School for Boys.

At that time it was during the War, just before D-Day. We knew very little of D-Day obviously. One day the Boulevard was full of lorries that were going across the channel, although we didn't know this at the time. Another day I was out for a walk with my mother and our dog and we went up to Belfairs Woods where there was a number of American lorries hidden amongst the trees. An American soldier called out to us "Would your little boy like these?" and it was a set of dominoes in a State Express cigarette tin. Then he said to my mother "These are no good to us where we are going, your little boy might like to play with them". I've still got them and me and my wife sometimes still play dominoes. Then one day we woke up and suddenly the lorries had all gone. That must have been something like June 6th 1944.

Earlier, in 1940, we were evacuated, bizarrely of all places to London, that was really so that my father could be near his job and partially because Southend was an expected invasion area. So we went up to London and rented a house in Muswell Hill and one night the roof got blown off it. So my father said "I've had enough of this. Let's go back to Leigh on Sea", which we did. We got to Fenchurch Street Station where the roof was still burning from the incendiaries the night before. We caught the train down to Leigh which was, surprisingly, running on time. We got down to somewhere like West Horndon and a plane was flying beside the train and we flung ourselves onto the floor thinking it was German and it might machine gun the train. But it was one of ours. Anyway we got back to Leigh and it was like a ghost town. I don't know what the capacity of Highlands Boulevard is, probably about 100 houses, and only about a dozen were being lived in by civilians. Many had been taken over by the army. Things were getting in a terrible state with weeds growing through the pavements and potholes but we felt much happier at Leigh and in any case it was established by then there wouldn't be an invasion. Hitler had lost out in the Battle of Britain and things carried on as normal.

The most obvious sign of the war at Leigh was that Leigh beach was barricaded off and probably mined. So our beach was by the cockle sheds further along where at least you could have a paddle and maybe a swim and dig among the cockle shells. There were a lot of children evacuated from Leigh so the only families living in Leigh were largely local government people whose jobs were here and who couldn't abandon them.

On VE day I came down to Old Leigh and there was a bonfire party going on where several complete boats were burnt, probably ones that had had their day and effigies of Hitler and all the rest of it. It was quite a party although alcohol played no part for me but probably did for mum and dad.

Our love of the sea and boats goes back to my grandfather who went round the world twice on sailing ships, originally as a cabin boy. After the first trip his father said I'm not having you in the lower deck in a ship and bought grandfather an indenture as an apprentice officer. He did a second trip but then ended up managing a bank in London and that was the end of his seagoing career. But he always had yachts at Westcliff and it was this that later prompted my father to move to Leigh as it was near Westcliff and the same stretch of water. For a while mother and father lived on their boat along the sea wall. This was very typical of the time and there were a number of old Thames Lighters nearby. The man who ran the area, Les Warland, had rowed them from up river, cut off the bows and turned them into little floating docks. One of them was designated his office and had a shed on it. The number of his employees varied between 12 and none depending on how his finances were. But Les was very good at record keeping and every boat that moved in that yard was recorded.

It was Les Warland who built my father his second boat. What father did was sell his house on Highlands Boulevard which produced enough money to buy a fisherman's cottage on Church Hill and used the rest of the money to have a boat built, which was actually illegal at the time. Wood was rationed like a lot of other things in 1948 and was not to be used for building pleasure craft. It could be used for fishing boats but not pleasure craft. So in great secrecy Islander was built in Les's Barges and I knew nothing of this until I was taken to see her in a half-planked up condition. Unfortunately I missed her actual launch as I was too busy train spotting at the time.

I kept a series of diaries between 1952 and 1954 with drawings of boats built in Leigh. There were a number of boat builders back then. Up the street next to the Customs House was a big tin shed. I don't know what it was originally for, possibly something to do with the war, but that was a boat builders run by a man called Eadie for some years. There was Johnson and Jago's of course, now Leigh Marina. There was also Seacraft which is now a restaurant. Johnson and Jago built two cockleboats the Vanguard and the Merlin. They built them at the same time alongside each other. Eadie's was mainly building yachts.

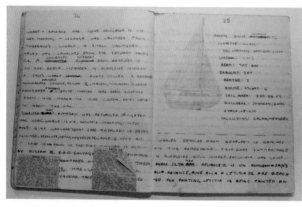

A page from Graham's diaries

My involvement with The Leigh Sailing Club came out of my father joining first. He really wanted nothing to do with Sailing Clubs or Yacht Clubs but one of his friends in the Crooked Billet was a member and persuaded him to go up there. He rather enjoyed himself so he decided to join it rather for drinking purposes if nothing else as it was cheaper than the pubs. Around about the same time my cousin got a sailing dinghy and I went sailing with him. We had ambitions to get bigger boats, both of us. Then we decided to join either Leigh Sailing Club or Essex Yacht Club. Well, we were more impressed with Leigh Sailing Club, it was friendlier to be honest, and so we joined there in 1953.

After that I started to work for the Port of London Authority. Later I had to go into

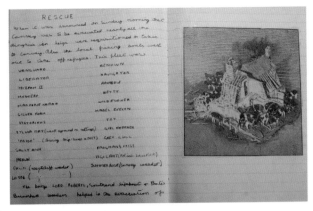

Graham's diary entry on the floods of 1953 which greatly affected places like Canvey Island and Foulness Island

the Navy for my National Service. But all the time I was saving to get this boat. Even in the Navy when I was on five shillings and sixpence a day I was still saving money towards a boat. Then I came out of the Navy and I had a bit of a windfall. I was summoned to the pay office before I left and they said "Able Seaman Dent we have realised we haven't been paying you sixpence a day RNVR money". I thought I don't think I'm entitled to this but I'm not going to disillusion this young WREN officer. So I said thank you as I picked it up and it came to about £17.00 so that went straight in the boat fund. So I eventually bought what was called a GB14 which was for £90.00 from someone in Thorpe Bay and that started off with a little adventure as we had to sail it from Thorpe Bay to Leigh around the pier.

The attraction to me of Leigh is the water. Also it is a good atmosphere in this town. It's like a big village really. I know about three or four hundred people who I can meet and have a coffee with. We had all the bother about the 'Road to the West' of course which meant the old town would have been flattened and the road would have run alongside the railway and that hung over us for a number of years. Southend Corporation had it all worked out so they thought. As far as the yacht clubs were concerned they thought they should combine and have just one clubhouse. But it wouldn't have worked as they were different clubs. Leigh Club was a fisherman's club to begin with and Essex's club was a business men's club. Some quite historic buildings were knocked down, but common sense has now prevailed and the old part of Leigh was saved.

JUNE SHARNICK (nee AXCELL)

I was born in 1931 in 3 Cliff Cottages, Billet Lane Leigh. I'm a pukka Leighite and I won't have anyone say that I'm not. If you are born in Old Leigh and your parents are born in Old Leigh you are a Leighite. Although my family originally came from Sweden in the 17th century. My brother in Australia has got a coat of arms which has a fish, a plough and a hammer on it.

I went to West Leigh Chapel for Sunday School and when I got older I had to go to the Evening Service and I ended up pumping the organ and I was supposed to get half a crown and my Dad's sister was in the congregation and they used to hand her the money instead of giving it to me and where would she go when she came out of church? The Crooked Billet Pub! My dad went mad. "The girl has pumped her bloody heart out" he said 'Pumping the organ so all you lot can sing and you go and spend her money in the pub".

My earliest memories of Leigh would be running up the back garden at the cottages because the toilet was up the yard. There was a wood and brick outhouse with a bath in it and we had to have a bath in there and mum would wrap blankets around us and run us back indoors. My mum was in service in one of the big houses off the Grand Drive and had a friend who she worked with who got a job in Leigh and then my dad and his friend Joe met up with them one night and they paired off.

My dad was Percy Axcell. He was taken from school at 11 by his father and was made to work on a cockle boat and that's how he learnt about engines. They didn't have all the glass partitions over the engine room they have now. My dad used to have to stand up in his Sou'wester, soaking wet.

June as a baby with her father

22

My father played for Leigh Ramblers Football Club. Most of them worked at Howard's Dairies, the milk people, they all played for them. His name was Percy but apparently when he was a footballer he used to weave in and out so they called him 'Snakey', others called him 'Steaky'

LEIGH RAMBLERS FOOTBALL CLUB 1932-33

G. Noakes, L. Emery, H. Harvey, A. French, W. Ripton, H. Armes, H. Thompson, F. Pearce, J. Hall. Trainer   J. Attwood, J. Gathercole, G. Johnson, C. Suttle, W. Banbridge   Secretary
Chairman   Captain   President   Vice-Captain   Vice-Chairman
R. Kerry, W. Deal, J. Richardson, P. Axcell

Leigh Ramblers Football Club   Percy is front row bottom left

His idol was Stanley Matthews. My dad would listen to a football match on the radio with his eyes closed shouting "Get it, get rid of the bloody thing". He was there in his mind. He taught himself to repair our shoes. It was always mine that had to be repaired as I was a bit of a Tom Boy. Some of the neighbours would come around and say 'Perce is there anything you can do with these?' and he would say 'Leave it with me, I'll see what I can do with them'. He was a good neighbour. If there was any problem people used to say "Get Steaky". My father also belonged to the Royal Order of Buffalos or The Buffs. They took the children on outings. Once a year on a Sunday the cocklers were allowed to take their families out on the boats and we would go to the other side, to Kent and we would play a game of football. We called them the 'yellowbellies'. I was very proud of my dad. When I used to walk down the cockle sheds they used to shout out 'Here comes young Steaky waiting for her dad.' And I would stay and bring my dad his food basket, with me.

The shed where the Heritage Centre is now, was the crushing shed for the cocklers where I used to watch them working. They used to take all the crushed shells in big lorries and take them to the building sites. I even had a cousin who made necklaces or earrings out of the cockleshells by painting them and selling them. Dad worked very hard. When we used to go out on the boat we would play in the mud and make castles and all that but Dad would work. Sundays as well he would do double shifts. Sometimes he would stay out for two days. If they were doing well they would stay until the boat was full and they would have a punt behind them which could be full of cockles too. It was all dependent on the tides especially when they are high tides, because a normal tide would come in soft but spring tides would double. So they would have to empty the boat quickly, go home and get more food and go back out. When he came in Mum would say "Oh dad, go to bed" and he would have a good wash and go straight to bed.

He had to put in for new thigh boots once as his old ones were leaking. And he came home one day and I was doing my homework at the table and I heard him say to mum "Can you have a look at it, it's very sore?" and mum shut the door and I heard her say "Oh Perce that looks painful". And the kettle went on and the salt and he had got a carbuncle and it was really painful. They worked in all weathers and wore oilskins. He would rub them with a type of oil and put them on a long pole and put them on the clothes line so they stiffened and became waterproof.

Then he would be up to London with the wheel barrow and sell cockles and winkles and jars of mussels. He took them to Barking most of the time. I used to have to go around looking for empty jam jars with the lids on down by the station. Mum would put them in boiling water to sterilise them. Then I used to have to get a big jar of vinegar and the mussels and cockles Dad had got would go in there, as well as shrimps and winkles, and he would stand and sell them outside the same pub in Barking every Sunday no matter what the weather was like. He would also walk into Southend sometimes to a shop; I think it was called Roberts which sold bags and I would sit and thread them on a string and Dad had them tied to the handles on his wheelbarrow and he had a pint mug and a half pint mug so he could sell them and measure them out to what the people wanted. Sundays we always had fish and the shrimps were my favourite. When he went up to Barking Dad would say "Can you do me a plate of winkles when I get home?" and I would have to sit there getting them out with a pin and putting them in a dish with some vinegar and that would be his tea when he came home.

Everyone in the family worked on the cockling or shrimping boats. My dad worked on the Renown and my brother and I were the last two children allowed to go on it before it got too bad during the war. He would have to ask the Commodore who was Mr Harvey or Mr Osborne if it was alright to take my brother or myself out because we were the only two children left in Old Leigh at that time.

You see my brother and I were the only two children not evacuated. My mum got us all ready and took us down the station. But we cried so much my mother brought us home. One mother said 'You are being cruel to those children.' And mum said, "Don't worry I'll put them out before the Germans get them".

Well we had a whale of a time being the only two children. We got into Plumbs Cottage and discovered we could get from one end of the cottages to the other because we found there were doors and they were papered over because of the people who would bring in contraband.

We were scrumping and we took the cabbages and carrots because there wasn't much money coming in and people had left allotments to move out of Leigh. We used to take the flowers as well because everything was left. We had favourite soldiers, English, Scots, Americans, Canadians and Czechoslovakian who gave us bars of chocolate. We also saw all the boats out there that went to Dunkirk and there were dogfights in the sky. We used to pick up shrapnel from the planes. The Germans also dropped bombs on their way to London.

My father continued to work as a fisherman during the war. He had to get what money he could, cos there was still the rent that had to be paid and things like electric and gas bills to pay. So when they got the all clear, the mine ship would go up the Thames after an air raid to check if there were any mines or bombs in the water. The boats would phone the end of Southend Pier where the military were all stationed and they would call down to Mr Osborne or Mr Harvey and say, yes you can go out.

My dad used to have a 20 foot punt and he used to go trawling with a net on a big metal ring. I can talk about this now because the war is over. During the war Dad got the OK to go out on his boat and when he got out to the end of the pier he dragged the net behind him. This black round thing came along with it and he thought I've got a mine. So he threw the anchor out and walked ashore to Chalkwell and told them he had got a mine in his net and when they came down they found it was actually a frogman, who had been killed or died, and the head had been caught in his net. We had the police around and they couldn't find his body so they didn't know if it was an Englishman or a German spy. But me and my brother had to swear on the Bible that we would never talk about it. It was very distressing for my father obviously.

We were watching the boats leaving for Dunkirk and stood up there and watched it. My dad was supposed to have gone but he was working for Fords at Dagenham. I think it was Mr Osborne or Mr Harvey who got in touch with Fords and told them

Dad was needed. He was so good with the motors so they trusted him with the engine. So they wanted him to go to Dunkirk but he was in a reserved occupation. But while he was on the train coming down there was a train travelling in the other direction on the same line and it stopped them getting through. My mother always blessed that train as it saved our dad because the boat he would have gone on was blown up. Two of his cousins were on the boat and as they were going out they saw Dad and they shouted out "Line 'em up Perce, Line 'em up. We'll see you when we get back". But they didn't come back, it hit a mine. He wouldn't speak to any of us for about a week because he felt he should have been on that boat too. He kept saying "I should have been on that boat".

At the end of the war there was a huge party in Old Leigh High Street on VE Day. I was sat at a table just outside the Crooked Billet. There were children there from Shoebury and all over the place. There were paste sandwiches I remember. Awful they were!

VE Day Party in Leigh (June is the girl with long dark hair on the right hand side at the back)

I went to Leigh North Street Primary School and I went up to West Leigh Secondary School until I was 14. Then I went straight to work in my uncle's place, he was a basket maker, he had a little shop in Church Hill and it was called The Basket Shop. His name was Tom Sage and we used to make children's and shopping baskets, things like the baskets that went on the front of bicycles. They were wicker baskets and we sat on the floor with big bits of wood over our legs. It was just the family, my two cousins and Uncle. The building is still there and some of the baskets at the Heritage Centre are just like some of the ones I made in the shop. Then I worked at the Pork Butchers at the top of the hill. So I went up in the world. It was called the Lincoln Pie Shop and we made Pork Pies and Sausages.

After that I got married and my parents had moved by that time to 4 Uttons Avenue. My mum would polish the letter box and keyhole every week. But we actually couldn't open the front door at all as it was so warped. When I had to get out to get to my wedding car I had to go out the back door and up an alleyway! The same thing happened when my dad died. Mr Thorpe, the undertaker, sent one of his workmen down to shave a bit off the door so we could get Dad's coffin out.

RON SVERDOFF

I was actually born in London. My parents were Southenders but, believe it or not, we moved to London during the war and my grandfather was a fireman during the Blitz. After the war we came back and lived at Fairfax Drive in Westcliff. We weren't a wealthy family and my father was a greengrocer come plumber! I remember him delivering all sort of orders coming up to Christmas on his trade bike. Everyone would invite him in for a sherry and he used to get back very late on Christmas Eve!

I grew up around this area and had associations with Leigh, although I didn't move into Leigh until the mid-1980s. When I was younger I was in the 3rd Chalkwell Bay Sea Scouts. I have very fond memories of the old railway station which now forms the opposite side of the Leigh Sailing Club. It was a staggered railway station and there was a level crossing there at the time and that was where we met. One of my happiest memories was going on wooding parties in the winter where we used to take a pram dinghy (a rowing boat) and collect driftwood to make fires in what we called The Den on the railway station. Health and Safety wasn't around in those days and the trains used to thunder past within elbows reach. There was no fence or railings and we were all youngsters. It was amazing no one was run down by the steam trains that came through. The sea scouts were run by a man who is held in great affection in Leigh called Frank Bentley. In fact he hasn't long passed away and there was a huge funeral procession just a few years ago. He ran the sea scouts for a long time. I was in the scouts in the late 1950s and he was still running the scouts into the 2000s. We did sailing of all types.

There were a lot of characters in Leigh. There was a man called Roger Giles. I wasn't a fisherman but I know if there was a problem with a boat's radar or electronics, whatever time of day or night, they would send one of the youngsters to knock on Roger's cabin door. He lived on an old Dutch tugboat around Bell Wharf. Whoever was sent to knock on his door was told to go away

Frank Bentley

rather brusquely shall I say. Then, after a couple of expletives, he would emerge from his hatch and he would always rally to the occasion, even if he told you to 'push off', or words to that effect. He smelt of greasy engine oil and his boat was a mess and when he sadly died I thought I had better dress up and go along, as I didn't expect many people would go. But the cortege went from the Mayflower Pub (then the Strand Cafe) right up over the flyover and back along New Road.

Another story concerning Roger also included my younger brother, Steve, who is a scientist with worldwide influence. Roger was also a very clever electronics engineer, quite how clever I hadn't realised. Well, my brother was coming to visit me and Roger was there helping to fit a kitchen for me. As Roger and I walked up to my house I saw a red Ferrari parked in my driveway and my heart sunk. My brother is something special to me, as Roger was, but I thought my brother wasn't going to get on with Roger, who smelt of oil and dressed a bit differently! Anyway as we walked through the back door I anxiously said 'Steve, this is my mate Roger'. Then they stared at each other and said "Roger?" "Steve?" and they both knew each other instantly. Apparently they had worked together at Echo Electronics on the nose cone of an Anson aircraft which had a prototype self-landing radar, which is still used today. I had no idea they knew each other and after that I couldn't separate them.

It can be dangerous around here on the water. You can get those sudden storms and then there are the mud flats and Maplin Sands where the War department fire guns. In fact I was nearly caught there. I was bringing a boat back from France for a local boat builder. We left early in the morning hoping to get to Rochford on the tide. I just plotted the quickest course as I knew it was possible to cut across the mud flats in the Estuary on a high spring tide. However we were halfway across the Maplin Sands, which I had forgotten was an exclusion zone, and we were almost in the River Crouch, when we saw all this smoke behind us. Then we realised they were firing guns over the top of us! I should have been miles round the other way.

I used to run the Queen of Kent in the 1980s. It was a ferry boat that ran from Southend Pier to Rochester and was licenced for 113 passengers and up to 7 crew. That was a nice little operation and I employed Dickie

Queen of Kent

29

Baldwin, a local fisherman, as skipper of that boat. Unfortunately it finished as it became uneconomical. Don Rose, who lived in Kent, owned the boat, but I was here in Southend to make sure passengers got on and off and it was re-fuelled and the provisions for the bar put on at Leigh.

I started 3 clubs in Leigh, a walking and cycling club, called the Traditional Touring Club, a rowing club, called The Lower Thames Rowing Club and The Scooter Club for people riding mobility scooters bought from my shop (Lifestyle and Mobility).

One of our rowing club events was a barbecue on Two Tree Island, or what I nicknamed Palm Island for the party. They had opened a new shopping centre in Southend called The Royals and they had these huge bronze palm trees for the opening. So I thought it would be nice to get a palm tree for my Palm Island and I saw these in a scrap yard and I asked the guy how much he wanted for it. He said 'You couldn't afford it' then I told him what we wanted it for and he said if we invited him then we could borrow it. So we had several boats ferrying this huge bronze Palm Tree onto the island so we could erect it and from the cliff tops you could see this great big palm tree sticking up from the tip of Two Tree Island. It looked spectacular!

We also had another party on the end of Canvey Point. It was an all-night party and all the local fishermen were out there. At dawn we had the candelabras on top of the piano, which was on fire, and yet the pianist continued playing it. We had some fun but we always cleared up we never left any debris behind. There was some criticism from the guests about the location at Canvey when the Liberty boat didn't come to take us home because it had a rope caught round its propeller and some of us were left on the island all night, which was fun when the tide came in round our ankles!

Obviously I have seen Leigh change. Leigh was famous in the old days for its cockles and winkles and people would come down from London to buy them as it was the nearest place to London they could get to the sea. Now it is very much a visitor or tourist town. But a lot of residents have family connections abroad. When the £10.00 passage came along many Leigh and London residents went to Australia, Canada or South Africa and now they come back as visitors and they remember their childhood days. So you get people taking pictures of odd things but its memory lane for them.

I live at Billet Wharf Cottage on Billet Wharf here in Old Leigh High Street. When it was owned by the Osbornes it was called the Salt Cottage and was derelict for many years. It was due for demolition because when the Leigh flyover was constructed they were going to knock the old town down. But local resistance brought many people out to stop it and I think Billet Wharf Cottage was the last one to be saved.

HAZEL HUNTER

My family were the Noakes family. My grandfather was William Noakes but he was known as 'Snappy' because I think he was a bit abrupt! There was a story that his father, John, had fallen off a sea wall and died while intoxicated. Snappy was born in Alley Dock which is at the back of the High Street. I think the house where he was born has been knocked down now because a lot of them were really just old huts. William lived in 19 High Street and he had a boatyard where he kept his boat the Silver Spray. That's where I remember him. In those days the fisherman all lived down here and I have to say anyone who lived up the hill was considered a foreigner.

William 'Snappy' Noakes and Jessie

Snappy's father was a fisherman too and he was fishing around the coast at Harwich where he met his wife. She moved back here and so did one of her sisters who also married into a fishing family so the family also stretches to Harwich.

Snappy was in the Merchant Navy during WW1. He was look out man and he saw a German torpedo coming towards the boat. He alerted the master to turn the ship away and in gratitude he was given £5.00 reward.

He served throughout the First World War and went all over the place with many trips to Brisbane and New York. I think sometimes they must have been troopships moving soldiers around.

Snappy and his wife met when my Nan came to work in service in Leigh. She was called Jessie Pickett and came from Laindon and they met and got married in St Clements. Then they had their children and war broke out and Granny was told to leave 'the water' and go and live in Laindon with her mum. My mum was married by then. So Granny took Walter my mum's brother and went there. But Grandad stayed here although I don't know what he did during the war. He was a 'Huffler' which was another name for a pilot who brought boats up the Thames. Later on after the war he had the boat called the Silver Spray. I remember he would go out on trips on that boat with about 20 children and mums going on visits to places like Walton on the Naze.

I believe after he was married he was offered a cottage on the Strand but he wouldn't take it as he was frightened my mum, who was still a little girl, would go out and fall in the water because it was all unprotected around the cottage.

Snappy taking out families for day trips on the Silver Spray

The first memory I have of him is when I was about 3 and he came to visit my gran when we were living at Laindon and he came to ask if she would move back with him. She had been down to Leigh earlier with her son, who was also my uncle of course. He was in his late teens and he looked around and said he didn't want to go into the fishing trade. So I think my grandad took umbrage and said "If you feel like that go back to Laindon and take him with you", so she did. So as I said he came to visit my gran to ask her to go back but when he saw my great-granny he said "She needs you more than me" and so he went back to live on his own at 19 High Street in Leigh.

William 'Snappy' Noakes of Leigh on Sea

When my other grandfather died in 1962, my mum and dad went to the funeral in Kent so granny came and brought me down to Snappy with my sister Vanessa, who was still in a push chair. I don't think he had ever seen Vanessa because he invited us in and made himself a cup of tea and sat down and he said to my granny 'Well you know where it all is help yourself.' It was really odd as he didn't offer to make her a cup of tea and he had this old tin of condensed milk which he used instead of ordinary milk and I was fascinated by it. I can remember meeting him up in The Broadway with mum later on. I was a teenager then and it was just before he died. I remember he was asking about my gran, his wife, as she had been poorly. He was actually very generous and he got out his wallet and took some money out and gave it to my mum to give to my granny.

Apparently he was a very popular character down here. He used to go to the pub when the holiday makers were down and he would sit at the bar and tell them all the tales of his life. He would sit with his cheese cap on and cigarette and they would buy him drinks.

He was a cockler and his brothers were too. Mum told me that when she was a little girl he would sell the cockles on little plates and she would have to wash them up. I can remember being down in Leigh one day and my grandfather's brother, John, coming along with a big bag of shrimps he had just boiled. But it was a very hard life for them all working on the boats.

One day a chap said to me, "I remember your grandad" and told me a story that at one time Snappy had to walk to Tilbury to pick up his boat and as he went he picked turnips out of the fields and ate them. Well, it would have been a fair old walk.

I'm proud of my story and I like my connection to Old Leigh. Downstairs in the Heritage Centre there's the names of all the mariners of Leigh and we have an ancestor that is on our family tree with the name Vandervord. He must have been Dutch and came over in the 16ᵗʰ century when they were building up Canvey Island and his name is on the list in the Heritage Centre. He was well known and later on one of his descendants built the first pier at Southend about 1829.

CHRISTOPHER BAILEY

My father's sister Grace was married to George Osborne, who had the nickname 'Pie'. He was the skipper of the Renown LO88. He was nicknamed 'Pie' I think after rhyme 'Georgie Porgey Pudden n Pie'. All the old town fishermen had nicknames of some sort. There was another one I remember called 'China' Cotgrove but they all had them.

The first Renown was the one destroyed on its return from Dunkirk in 1940 and George Osborne lost his brother and his cousin on board along with a naval rating. Then they had the second Renown built during the war. But that was found to have too much draught and so it was too big to go in and out of the creek. Then they had Renown 3 which was in use up until the 1980s when they replaced it with another Renown called Renown 4. When George retired his son Trevor took over the Renown and they had Renown 5. These were all cockling boats. Although the second Renown actually wasn't suitable for cockling and I saw it off Ramsgate Harbour in the 1980s where it had been converted into a cruising boat and was called Renowned.

I used to spend a lot of time at the Osborne house as a child with all the cousins. I didn't live in Leigh for part of my childhood but I came to stay with my grandparents in the summer and would go out regularly on the Renown. I would be on the boats while they were cockling.

There would be a group of about 8 men on aboard and they would go over the side when they reached the cockle ground. The boat would then dry out on the mud and the men would climb down and rake the cockles out of the mud into a net, wash them, put them into a basket and when they had filled two baskets they would carry them back to the boats with a yoke. So in that way they would gradually fill up the hold and when the tide came in they would all be back on-board and come back to Leigh. It was hard work for the men and I think they were paid by the size of the catch. As children, of course, we were just there having fun.

The Osbornes still have the cockle shed by the Crooked Billet and they were one of the big cockling families of Leigh. There used to be a lot of cockle sheds selling cockles between the Crooked Billet and all the way up to the station. But most of those have gone and the sheds are just used for processing rather than selling.

But when I was a child there was always the fishy smell as they were cooking the cockles. They cooked the cockles in their shells and then put them in a griddle and shook them. The cockles would then fall out of the shells and the shells would be shot out onto the forecourt outside the sheds into a big heap to be taken away later. Then the cockles were kept in salted water and sold on their stall in the front. There were also Shrimp boats at that time and that was a lovely smell as they sometimes cooked the shrimps on the boat as they sailed back. They don't have many Shrimpers now.

There was also a time where they had whitebait boats and white weeding boats. It was a weed that only grows around here and they would collect it and dry it and colour it and use it for decoration. Shellfish was very important to this community.

In those days there would be half a dozen boats or more going out at the same time to the cockle grounds. There was also a lot of inter-marriage among the families as everyone knew everybody else.

Later the wooden ships changed to steel boats. That was when they started to get grants from the EU and they could get money to build steel boats. The steel boats were better for dredging as they had bigger engines and more deck equipment which they had to have to suck up the cockles from the seabed.

One year I went on the Trawler race that used to start at one side of the pier then down the other side and back to the pier head. The boats would race as fast as they could go. I think we came second. They were all the fishing boats from Leigh and some of the fishing boats from Southend. It was very competitive and the boats would be decorated with flags and banners. Apart from the regular crews they would have friends and family on-board cheering and waving. I was on the Renown Three, the Osborne's boat. The boats always raced under power rather than sail and would try to get the biggest engine.

My family weren't directly involved in the fishing industry although my father was a fishmonger. He had two shops in London and they sold fish and chips. One shop was in Poplar and then he moved to Forest Gate. After he died in the 1960s we sold the shop in London and my mother opened a shop selling Children's Clothes in Rectory Grove, Leigh. I was 14 in 1958 when I came back to Leigh from London. I did notice things like the lack of traffic in Leigh compared to London and I could cycle five miles along the Southend Arterial road each day there and back to go to school.

The other side of my family was my mother's and her grandfather was Charles Jacobs. He moved to Leigh after the First World War. They lived in different places but one of them was in one of the old coastguard cottages just along past the station on the other side of railway. He worked for Leigh Building Supply and in those days there were horses and carts. Leigh Building Supply also owned the Timber Wharf in the old town here where they would bring in all the building supplies for the houses they were building in Leigh at that time.

Obviously I have seen the slow decline in the fishing industry over the years in Leigh. I think the major change was when they changed the type of cockle fishing from manual labour to the dredgers. They had smaller crews then and the boats went out at different times. When they did the raking the boats went out on the tide so they could dry out now they go out as the tide rises and come back as the tide goes out. It's surprising how many of the cockle boats got stuck in the creek as they left too late. In the 1920s they dug the creek out as it silted up. I remember the cockle boats often dragging a chain behind them so it would stir up the mud and it would flow out on the tide. So it had an automatic dredging effect. The creek was much deeper then than it is now. I believe there are suggestions that they are going to dredge the creek again to make it deeper as it is silting up again.

In 1959 I joined the Leigh Sailing Club when I was about 15. Just before that I had built a sailing dinghy from a kit and that was why I joined the club. I learnt to sail there and I have been a member ever since. I was Club Secretary for a number of years and then Vice Commodore and Commodore. So I have quite a long history there and although I don't sail anymore we do use the club socially.

Chris Bailey at Bell Wharf

The biggest change in my lifetime has been the decline of the fishing industry and there is less retail down here now. A lot of the catch is sent away to be sold elsewhere. The old town has changed and some of the old buildings were destroyed in the 1950s and 1960s. The old railway crossing

Preparing dinghies for sailing in Bell Bay 1959

had to be changed when the rails became electrified and we had a new bridge. The High Street in Old Leigh has changed. It is more of a visitor centre with so many restaurants and cafes and people come from far and wide to visit, especially at the weekends when you can sometimes hardly walk along here.

MAURICE GEORGE DEAL

My ancestry is a real history of local fishing linked with famous families like Wilder, Gilson, Ashman, Turner, Boyton, Britton, Shaw and Noakes.

My great Grandmother was Eliza Osborne and my great grandfather was Henry Wilder (born 1836). My grandmother was Jane Eliza Wilder and my Grandfather was Robert John Deal (1858 – 1940)

Robert spent all his life on the water as he fished for cockles. They used to cook them onboard, until there was a cholera outbreak and the authorities stopped them preparing the cockles on the boats and made them prepare cockles in the sheds. Later he used to run day trips on the "Happy Home", he was a really hard worker.

Grandad often helped with teaching children in the Sea Scouts how to tie knots. They lived at No 1 Bell Cottages and 11 children were born there. Jane's family lived at No2 and I remember as a child sitting in a room playing with a toy listening to these adults talking. I remember Robert well. We had lots of local families like the Osbornes and the Meddles around us at all times. Old Itty Meddle use to play darts with my dad, when dad wasn't playing footy that is.

My mother was Nellie Knibb and my father was George Deal (1895-1961). They were a strange combination, but they met in the newly built "Empire Theatre" in 1915 when he was on leave from the army. They married in 1925, in Quainton, but lived in Cranleigh Drive, I think. They had two boys 6 years apart. Maurice George on 10 May 1935 (me) and Michael Robert on 14 May 1941.

I went to Chalkwell Junior School in Southend and then I went to Fairfax School when I was about 10 or 11 years old. After my exams i was offered a scholarship at Municipal College in Southend. When I was 13, there were 30 odd boys learning building and the same for engineering. It was a 3 year course but after 2 years it was clear it was costing too much money for the equipment for joinery, so I asked to leave to go to work. My dad was only earning £9 a week for plastering, and work wasn't regular... times were hard then.

So at 15 years of age dad took me to meet his old school friend Len Johnson. Len said I needed to apply myself properly at Johnson and Jago's Yard. So first thing on a Monday morning in Autumn 1950 I started sweeping up, working with joiners, helping them to make their door hatches, riveting and helping on 18-22 foot sloops (that was a sailing boat with 1 mast, and a steel turner engine).

By 1951 I had moved to the big shed, now helping with 23-26 foot cabin cruisers, mostly these were used on the Thames, but some were narrow enough to go on canals.

But no one was buying boats after the war. Len had to make 40% of his qualified staff redundant and took on cheaper staff.

Then I met an old friend called John Knapp. He had been in local fields 'gleaning' for his ducks, whilst I was out 'gleaning' for chickens. John and I had known each other since we were children. I was working at Jago's and John Knapp joined me there later. Later on the senior boys including John and I were put onto bigger boats, or promoted if you like, because the sales team had sold lots of orders at the boat show in 1952.

It was also around this time I lost my front tooth while boat building. I was covering for an old boy who had gone to hospital and putting the last plank in and it was very tight fit. I was 15 foot up on scaffolding and the "young boy" working with me called Fazakerley hit the plank. It came up too quick, hit me in the chops and knocked

me clean off top and I ended up out cold on floor.

I qualified as a shipwright 1955 and my call up to National Service was deferred until I was qualified. So in February 1956 I went into the army and I left in September 1957.

Mo Deal on John and Colin Knapp's Boat 1953

I went back to Johnson's who kept my job open for me. I was doing odd days when the weather was too bad for the sea. At that time I was going out to collect white weed on a boat called the Cornucopia with Colin Knapp. Michael (my brother) had already started his 5-year apprenticeship 1956, when he was 15. Later I was to take Snappy Noakes out in the same way Colin had done with me.

When Frederick Jordon who was known as 'Whiplash' bought a boat called Merlin, which was made at Johnsons, I was headhunted as skipper. Colin Knapp came with me we started towing jobs. We also leased Victoria Wharf from Turnidge the sailmakers and started our own boat building yard. There was John and Colin Knapp, Michael and me and we got an order for cheap cabin cruiser in 1960-61 from Grant Jones.

Then in 1962 I bought 1st Kestrel from Albert.V.Jackson working from Peterborough. It was a wooden boat and I rebuilt her with John and Michael. Me, Micheal, John and Colin were all good friends and we often went out together. One night we were at a dance where I met my wife Daphne. She was beautiful, and a good dancer! She was friends with Bob's wife to be, Iris. We married June 1964 and honeymooned on Isles of Scilly.

By 1964 I had changed work again. I was refueling and working boats for Roy Bates. He ran the Radio Essex pirate station from the Sea Forts. These were defensive forts built out at sea during the Second World War. The Fort he took over was called the Knock John Tower.

I did lots of towage work over next few years. There were some days the weather was terrible; I'm not sure if I was very lucky or very skilled. There were huge waves crashing down around me. You could always feel the storms coming in, the wind would blow really hard out at sea and it changed the nature of the waves so towing large objects too was very difficult.

In 1966 I started working at Allied Mills for Mr Tucker and Dave Allen on the River Roach in Rochford towing in huge ships to unload. It was 24-hour callout, so in the early days with 2 children I could be up all night with the tides. I then needed to register at Port Customs at 9am in the morning! At one time there was a Dock Strike and fourteen ships were waiting at Paglesham and we managed to get everything logged in on one tide. I was ferrying customs chaps back and forth.

Around 1968, I was working at Leigh piloting ships. It was at this time in 1975 that I sold my boat Eugenio to Chris Thompson. I continued in some of my jobs and bought the Steel Kestrel as a part exchange. She eventually sunk at Rochford, and I bought a boat called Kingfisher in 1984. This was my last boat and in 1985 I sold her.

Whilst working fishing parties at Leigh around 1975 I met Mick Headford, the boat he was racing was sinking and I helped him back to shore. Mick had a pony called

'Rocky' and I offered to help him out. The pony was housed opposite the end of the runway at Southend Airport. In those days there were lots of stables and farms near the airport before it was extended. One day Rocky bolted and ended up running onto the runway but I managed to catch him pretty quickly.

Soon I had my own horse Sarina, she was a Piebald Mare and she was housed same place as Rocky. I used to ride her home to Southchurch regularly, but one evening in 1979 I was driving her home in the cart and she bolted. She ran across Southchurch Boulevard. I thought 'you go!' and I jumped out before the end of Arlington. But I caught my ankle in the wheel and she dragged me for a while! She left the cart between two Cherry trees, and grazed on a nice lawn till someone took her to some local stables. I was out cold for a while. I was eventually put into full leg cast for six weeks with three screws and metal rod for broken tibia and fibula. There wasn't a lot of money for us, so I had to go back to work. It was difficult on a boat on your own when you are driving and piloting with more stairs to go up and down especially after the accident and I was still looking after the horse with my injury.

During the next 10 years Sarina had 2 foals, Robert and Elizabeth. We also had some calves from time to time, and lots of chickens (home breeding) as well as cats and dogs. There were newly built stables, with Michael and my daughter Susan's help near the Southend Boundary A127 Progress Road. We drove both foals, most weekends.

Then I met Graham Collins through the blacksmith. He wanted rebuild the "Howards Dairy Cart". It was to contain all the original parts and I ended up building two of them! We built them for the Regents Park Easter Parade in 1984. Graham, his horse Ted and I attended. Ted pushed through the crowd and ate a child's ice-cream that her carer was holding at the time. The next year 1985, which was the Centenary year I drove my own horse Robert and my daughter Susan in the parade. After that I started gardening and had a few contracts - some big and some small jobs.

I worked with Graham at Collins Dairy, maintaining milk floats and odd jobs and carried on till I retired due to ill health 2014. My hip was dislocating, so sold my land and animals. Then my wife broke her hip at about the same time, so she needed care.

Between the years of 2002-2005 I worked on and off on the boat Endeavour with Peter Wexham. He asked me to caulk the boat, when it was kept at Great Totham. So I would drive up with my grandson George and we spent the days making the rudder for her and caulking to make her water tight. Later when she came back to Leigh, I was asked to fit the bowsprit for the sails. I am in the process of donating tools for her restoration again now.

THE ROAD TO THE WEST

From an interview with three of the campaigners: **Jane Lovell** (JL) **Alan Crystall** (AC) and **Margaret Buckey** (MB) carried out by David Savill (DS) from Age Exchange

Left to Right: **Jane Lovell, Alan Crystall, Margaret Buckey**

JL

I came to Leigh-on-Sea as a complete outsider in 1964. My Husband had got a job at Thurrock Technical College and we wondered where to live. I looked at a map of the estuary and saw 'Bay' at Thorpe Bay, so I decided to take a train right through the area. On the way I saw this old village-y place and I thought, "Well that looks interesting, so we'll go to Leigh-on-Sea". Two days later we came down and over a weekend we bought a house here. So we were coming to Leigh-on-Sea and I knew no one. In 1966 I had a child, a girl. By this time I was very much anchored to the area because of having children. But I became very lonely and isolated. I met one friend, called Lettie, who'd got two older children. She used the Leigh swimming pool which was like a youth club. Then we heard that it was to shut and I became very angry on her behalf really. I thought this shouldn't happen. This is a very local facility. People could use it. It was free. Everybody could walk to it, all the children came down. It was safe, it was sea water. There were no expenses to it. I thought, "This is outrageous". So I wrote a letter to the paper and thought if anybody gets in touch with me I'll carry on and somebody did. It was the leader of the Leigh swimming club. So we got together and planned what to do. We went to the local rate payers meeting which existed then and brought it up with Mike King, who was the Chairman at the time. And he said we could address the Council to reverse the decision. He was very kind and he took me to rehearse our presentation in the Council chamber. Then the lady from the swimming club came with me to address the council and the decision was reversed in favour of keeping the pool open. So I thought "Thank God!". Then two years later, there became a threat to Jocelyn's Beach. By this time I had had another child, a little boy. They wanted to put left over clay from work on an overflow sewage pipe on it. They'd been left with a huge amount of clay so they wanted to use it to make a car park on the beach! It was actually from the Prittle Brook Relief scheme. The Prittle Brook overflow had flooded and it was a problem year after year. It would flood people's houses. So they thought the answer was to build a huge tunnel from there to Jocelyn's Beach and with all the masses of clay they thought, build on Jocelyn's Beach and let's have a car park.

I thought this was the final environmental idiocy. You destroy what you are coming to by getting a car to get here. So I was really angry by this time. I didn't know what to do. At that time I still didn't know many people really. So I took my pram and my toddler down to the beach and set up a card table to collect signatures. I thought then that's all I could do to try and stop the beach being lost.

Campaigning on the beach near Chalkwell Station

There was a Councillor who represented Chalkwell for a long time. He came up to me and said "This beach is my business". Told me I should take my nose out of it and leave. But I didn't. So I carried on collecting signatures and at that point everybody in the area had become completely aware of this threat because there were letters in the newspaper and everything else. And then the big campaign started. The Liberals called a meeting in the Catholic Church on the Leigh Road. People were pouring in, sitting on window sills, or waiting outside. Everyone stayed for the entire meeting. I have never seen a meeting like it. It was totally incredible. A committee was elected. I was late, I was teaching, but somebody had said "Well what about her (that's

42

me)?" People had noticed me collecting signatures I suppose. So I came on the committee. We made a large banner and car stickers. The car stickers were a massive campaign at that point. They were bright green and they changed design about every month. We put a different slogan on it like "Save our beach" or "No road through here". You went round Leigh and one in every two cars were covered in car stickers in the back window. My favourite car sticker was "No road to the West". At this point I had become the Press Secretary of the Leigh-on-Sea Sea Front Action Group. It was really like having a full-time job. I was on the phone for a much of the day for months. It became a job. Also by this time I was running a play group, so it I was now really rooted in Leigh-on-Sea. It became my place if you like. From not knowing anybody to knowing a lot of people here. So we made banners, car stickers, there were meetings, a press campaign. Myself and another person on the campaign, Mary Anderson, wrote the front page of the local paper, the Southend Standard at least twice. We wrote the front page for them and they just printed it. And the campaign was growing all the time. People stopped us, if you were handing out stickers, people would stop in the road and ask' "Can I have one?" Which was really good. We did beach clean ups. We were packed out at all the meetings, all over the area. It was a massive, massive campaign. My view was that if you added up all these local little bits of action....if people like us didn't protect our little beach, then there wouldn't be any beaches left for anybody, anywhere in this country.

I just want to say one more little thing. This massive campaign became a campaign about stopping the Road to the West which was a proposed road from the western end of Chalkwell Esplanade joining up with the A13 through Leigh and Hadleigh. Around 1914 the County Borough of Southend, as it was then, had promised Leigh that the seafront road would be continued from Chalkwell through Old Leigh. So Southend Council were proposing to deliver on this original promise, albeit in different times. We became aware that the Council was working to remove the obstacles to The Road to the West. The swimming pool was in the way of the road. The beach was in the way of the road. So we decided that if we didn't fight The Road to the West, we would have continual stupid battles all the way along.

AC

We moved to Southend, to Thorpe Bay in 1943. It was a restricted area then. My father was a cabinet maker. He had lost his right thumb on a wood-working machine. So he couldn't hold a rifle. So he was an ARP warden during the War. He patrolled in the City of London right through the Blitz. It was just like the front-line really. But in 1943, he got a licence to move into Thorpe Bay. I was about eight when we arrived.

And at that time the whole of the seafront all the way from Shoebury was cordoned off with barbed wire, right through Leigh-on-Sea too. The only place you could get to the water was a little gap in Old Leigh to the west side of Bell Wharf. There was a little narrow gap there, which is where in the wartime I saw the sea trials of the Water Buffalo which were used at D-Day.

I cycled down to Old Leigh one time in the War and I remember seeing troops. You could go along the promenade of Thorpe Bay but not anywhere here in Old Leigh. As a child Old Leigh seemed very pretty to me. There were little houses with flowers outside. It was great. So many years later when I heard about the campaign to save Old Leigh, and the beach etc, I got involved. My involvement came through my wife Elaine joining as she was already active. Mary Anderson wrote a big letter in the Southend Standard. My wife saw the advert. "Do you want a car park on Jocelyn's beach? If you don't, phone this number". So she did and we became part of the campaign group with Jane and Mary Anderson and a whole crowd of people.

I felt very strongly about being involved. There was a line on the map and the council owned all the buildings I think apart from the pubs. They owned every building in the Old Town. They had bought everything you see and, Jocelyn's Beach was the first bit they saw a way of coming right the way through from Shoebury Common. That was the plan, to take the major road into Southend along the seafront. My wife and I were involved in the committee. We had meetings all the time. Plotting and saving. We had a huge jumble sale and we raised £200 which in those days was a huge amount. Yes, there was enormous support.

Mobile campaigning

MB: It took over our lives didn't it? It literally took over our lives.

DS: So Margaret, you were recruited by Alan's wife, Elaine

MB

Elaine and I had been at school together and knew one another. My husband moved down here as a boy, when he was about one. I was introduced to the idea that you put a tent up on Chalkwell Beach usually the night before and then next day you'd spend all day down on the beach. So when I heard about Jocelyn's Beach being made into a car park, Elaine just recruited me and said "Margaret will you come to a meeting?" I was a shorthand secretary, I could do shorthand typing so I was quite happy to do the minutes. They are all upstairs in the Heritage Centre now, the whole lot of the action group archive is there.

MB: We had a very strong Leigh Residents Association.

JL: It was the rate payers that I first went to.

MB: It was so emotional. Young families here that used the beach...it became a very dominant factor in our life in Leigh, the fact that this road was going to be built. North Street School was important in our campaign. It helped because parents whose children were there got involved. And so that started as a focal point where you could recruit mums in the playground. Having children the beach was such an important factor. It was so important in my life. We used to spend all our summers on Chalkwell Beach and Jocelyn's Beach.

AC: I admired Mike King. He was a local Councillor. I liked the way he worked and he influenced me and eventually I said "I want to become a Councillor like you". He said "No you don't do you?" So that's how I got involved from a Council point of view later on. The action group called a meeting and Father Dan Shanahan (he was the Priest at the Parish Church, a wonderful man) let us use the hall for free. He was very supportive, and that meeting was the most amazing meeting. We had three Councillor's on the platform and they didn't know whether they were coming or going. Mike King who chaired the meeting said that was the most amazing meeting he had ever chaired. He just felt it was so powerful, the atmosphere was absolutely amazing. That was a hugely important meeting against the Road to the West. It really raised the temperature. It was packed, people were having to stand outside.

MB: Autumn 68.

DS: Margaret, having spoken to you before, are you still swimming at Jocelyn Beach?

MB: Yes. Well, it goes right back doesn't it really to when we saved that road.

JL: You were probably swimming there before then.

MB: We looked on it as our beach didn't we really?

AC: And we rented a locker space from the council. We had to buy our own tent to put up on the beach. And I used to curse every Sunday morning. I'd get up about 6 because to go and put the tent up because if you didn't get there in time there wasn't room to put the tent up.

MB: That's right, you'd spend all day down there.

JL: I never used anything but Jocelyn's Beach and I never had a tent. Had my own particular place on Jocelyn's beach and went there every day.

AC: The railway wall, it used to get hot in the sun and reflect the heat back. There was around forty regulars so it was a group of us.

DS: And I suppose the next bit of the story is, when did you succeed? What was the mark of success? How long did it all take?

MB: 76. Was it 76?

AC: It succeeded when the County Council took that line off the map. And Mike King was involved in that.

DS: Literally took the road off the map?

AC: Yes.

MB: Well it was the group that arranged to get that clay from that beach. It was Eugene Christie and Mike King, and another Councillor? They met didn't they? They got it (the clay) taken over onto Two Tree Island, to raise the sea wall over there.

AC: Raise the level of the land.

JL: I think they took the clay away from the beach around 1971 but probably the road didn't come off as a plan until 1976

MB: '76.

JL: Being nominally still Chairman, the Council still contacts us regarding planning issues asking 'What do we think?' It is quite useful as there are only four of us left now with £8 in the bank. Nevertheless we still raised a demonstration around 2012 against the building of a hospice on Hadleigh Downs

MB: When they took the Road to the West off, Grace Robson was a Councillor, and once the road was taken off, it became the third conservation area.

DS: So the road is removed from Council plans?

MB: Yes.

DS: So was the Leigh Society a way of formalising the response to what had happened with the action group? I mean was it a way of saying we need something permanently in place.

JL: I think it was in a way, yes. It was a continuation of the conservation areas that had already been started up the hill, which came down into the Old Town.

AC: There was a second conservation area and a third area at Leigh Cliff. So it was gradually revolutionised. The Old Town conservation area. Leigh Cliff conservation area.

MB: Once the road was totally removed from plans, that was when they actually then created this conservation area. But we got involved with so many threats. We got involved with oil refineries. They wanted to build another oil refinery. We got involved with Canvey residents. Then there was the Hadleigh Castle Country Park which is there now, well that was going to be built on. The Salvation Army owned that land. So we got involved with all these campaigns.

JL: And Thames Estuary Airport. We went to a big meeting on that and they were fighting it from the Shoebury end.

MB: And then we fought what was called a 'marina' off Two Tree Island. Really a housing scheme as most marinas are!

AC: Yes it was a housing scheme with a marina attached.

DS: So do you feel that you have always had to fight, to keep the place intact?

All: Yes, we have.

MB: We've fought for what we've got.

JL: I feel that it is under permanent attack.

AC: I was Councillor for Leigh Ward for forty years, and I never ever lost my seat because we were always fighting, for the public.

MB: Well I think it had atmosphere here. You used to come down here for big firework displays. They had bonfires all the way along. It was always a place with atmosphere. The pubs were the most popular thing. And the cockle industry. People used to come down and get their shrimps and winkles. It was a thing. My family, my father, relatives used to come down on Saturdays, and the major thing was to go down to Old Leigh to the cockle sheds and buy winkles, shrimps, Old Leigh shrimps, the brown shrimps. Well there were whelks and things. Jellied eels. You know, Old Leigh was a London destination on the train for people from the East End to come to Old Leigh and get their shell fish.

AC: You got off the train in Leigh and you were here, in the heart of it.

MB: And then you've got the river, The Ray. When the tide goes out, in the summer, you walk out there to The Ray and swim out there. That's another big thing, isn't it? You walk out and play cricket out there on the mound.

JL: It's like another whole area – difficult and quite dangerous to get to, but worth it. It's quiet and you could be anywhere in the world on hard compacted sand.

MB: My husband used to carry me over the muddy bit because some of the mud was rather soft and you put your feet through onto cockle and mussel shells.

DS: So this is only for people who know what they are doing?

All: Yes.

JL: It was a long walk. So it was a whole Sunday morning to walk there and walk back. And that to me was what was marvellous about the area and still is. And the funny thing is when they were doing repairs somehow to the bridge they blocked off the cinder track for two or three weeks, and people were just climbing over the barricades. They just wouldn't have it.

JL: My son comes down daily, well nearly daily, to swim off Jocelyn's. He takes his three year old son, well he's taken him since he was born, down there. He's on Jocelyn's Beach all the time.

DS: And is it the same thing for your family Alan, do they feel the same connection?

AC: Oh yes, absolutely. My son is now a Green Councillor. He's followed his father being on planning committees.

DS: And as a result of what you all did hundreds and thousands of people continue to enjoy this very beautiful place each year. Last question. I'll ask it to each of you.

Are you proud of what you did, to save this place?

JL: Yes, I think it's probably the best thing I ever did in my life, so far.

AC: Yes, it was an important part of my life and it continued on to the Council where I could do other things that benefitted so yes, it's a growing, it's a moving forwards all the time, yes.

MB: Yes, I can't help but feel proud really when you see the result of all the school children come to the Heritage Centre to learn about the history of the area. And the number of people who come from abroad who sign our visitors' book here in the Heritage Centre. They just love it, don't they?

JL: Can I just say one more word. For me, it's gone on to be part of a big environmental crusade.

All: Yes.

AC: We think we've won the major battles now

ACKNOWLEDGEMENTS

We would like to thank everyone who gave their time and shared their stories. This includes all of the contributors to this book and others including the volunteers at Leigh Heritage Centre.

Thank you to Carole Mulroney and Jennifer Simpson for supporting the whole 'Revealing the Maritime History of Leigh-on-Sea' project, including accessing the Heritage Centre's archives, and Ed Simpson for helping with logistics. Thank you to the volunteers who helped with the project including the open sessions, finance and in project meetings – Audrey Stirling, Cathy Cottridge, Dec Mulroney, Jackie Jackson-Smith, Trevor Matthews and Bernard Hetherington.

Thank you to Sue Wood for all the input and advice on the Mo Deal story. Thank you also to other family members who have helped with clarifications.

Thank you to Tim Hinchliffe for photography support throughout.

Thank you also to Thames Estuary Partnership, the lead organisation for the North Thames Fisheries Local Action Group (NTFLAG) programme, and everyone who took part through the NTFLAG Board.

We would like to thank our funders
- European Maritime and Fisheries Fund, managed by the Marine Management Organisation
- National Lottery Heritage Fund
- Southend-on-Sea Borough Council

'Front Cover Picture: William (Joe) Deal fishing on his boat the Endeavour in the 1960s'